Places in American History

The Statue of Liberty

by Susan Ashley

Reading consultant: Susan Nations, M.Ed., author/literacy coach/consultant

WEEKLY WR READER
EARLY LEARNING LIBRARY

Please visit our web site at: www.earlyliteracy.cc
For a free color catalog describing Weekly Reader® Early Learning Library's
list of high-quality books, call 1-877-445-5824 (USA) or 1-800-387-3178 (Canada).
Weekly Reader® Early Learning Library's fax: (414) 336-0164.

Library of Congress Cataloging-in-Publication Data

Ashley, Susan.
      The Statue of Liberty / by Susan Ashley.
          p. cm. — (Places in American history)
      Includes bibliographical references and index.
      Contents: The light of Liberty — A gift from France — A grand statue — Statue of Liberty facts —
Visiting the Statue of Liberty.
      ISBN 0-8368-4143-3 (lib. bdg.)
      ISBN 0-8368-4150-6 (softcover)
      1. Statue of Liberty (New York, N.Y.)—Juvenile literature.   2. New York (N.Y.)—Buildings, structures, etc.—
Juvenile literature. [1. Statue of Liberty (New York, N.Y.) 2. National monuments.] I. Title. II. Series.
      F128.64.L6A84   2004
      974.7′1—dc22   2003062113

This edition first published in 2004 by
Weekly Reader® Early Learning Library
330 West Olive Street, Suite 100
Milwaukee, WI 53212 USA

Editor: JoAnn Early Macken
Art direction, cover and layout design: Tammy Gruenewald
Photo research: Diane Laska-Swanke

Photo credits: Cover, title, pp. 7, 9, 11, 14, 19 National Park Service, Statue of Liberty National Monument;
pp. 4, 21 © Eugene G. Schulz; p. 5 Kami Koenig/© Weekly Reader Early Learning Library, 2004; pp. 6,
8, 12, 13 © North Wind Picture Archives; pp. 10, 15, 16, 18, 20 © Gibson Stock Photography

Printed in the United States of America

1 2 3 4 5 6 7 8 9 08 07 06 05 04

Table of Contents

The Statue of Liberty rises above
New York Harbor.

The Light of Liberty

The Statue of Liberty is one of the largest statues
in the world. It is also one of the most famous
statues. It shows a woman wearing a crown and
a flowing robe. She holds a torch high above her
head. The torch represents the light of liberty.

The statue stands on a small island in New York Harbor. The island is called Liberty Island. It is near Manhattan in New York City. The Statue of Liberty greets people coming to the United States. It has been a sign of welcome for more than one hundred years.

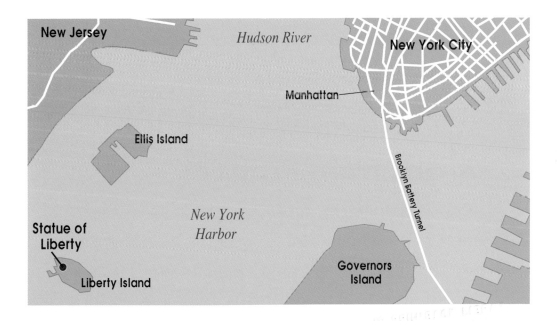

British troops fought American soldiers
during the Revolutionary War.

A Gift from France

France helped the American colonies during
the Revolutionary War. France helped them
win independence from Great Britain. The war
lasted from 1775 to 1783. The people of France
shared the Americans' love of freedom.

The two countries became friends. One hundred years later, France gave the United States a gift. The Statue of Liberty was a birthday gift. People in France raised money for the statue. They wanted their gift to represent freedom. They wanted it to show the friendship between the United States and France.

The Statue of Liberty was a gift of friendship.

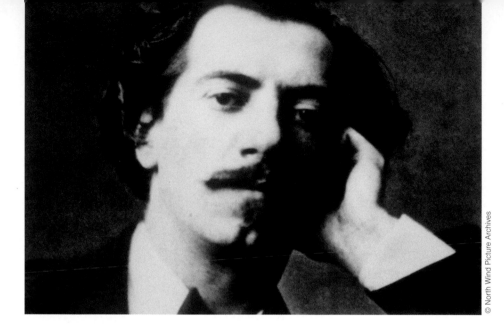

Frederic-Auguste Bartholdi
designed the Statue of Liberty.

A French sculptor named Frederic-Auguste
Bartholdi designed the statue. Bartholdi went to
New York. He chose the site for the statue. He
could picture a large statue standing on the island.
He returned to France and got to work.

Workers in France began to build the statue in 1875. The statue was so big that it had to be built in pieces. The hand holding the torch was the first piece to be built. It took hundreds of workers ten years to finish the statue.

To make the statue's hand, French workers first made a wooden mold.

The outside of the statue is made of copper. Copper is not as heavy as other metals. It is easy to bend. The copper is like the statue's skin. It is about as thick as a quarter.

The statue is covered with thin sheets of copper.

Beneath the copper skin is a steel skeleton. The skeleton supports the statue just like your skeleton supports your body. A Frenchman named Gustav Eiffel designed the Statue of Liberty's skeleton. He later became famous for building the Eiffel Tower in Paris.

The statue was built piece by piece.

The statue was finished in 1885. Then it had to be shipped to New York. It was too big to ship in one piece. Workers took it apart. They packed each piece in a crate. The crates were sent to New York. Then the statue had to be put back together again.

Crowds cheered when the French ship carrying the statue arrived in New York.

A Grand Statue

The statue was unveiled on October 28, 1886. The people in New York City celebrated. More than one million people watched a parade. The president gave a speech. Boats filled New York Harbor. Everyone wanted to see the statue. At night, fireworks lit up the sky.

The Statue of Liberty was cause for celebration.

Millions of people were moving to the United States. They came from other countries. For many of them, life had been very hard. They came to the United States to find a better life.

The Statue of Liberty was a symbol of hope for people coming to the United States.

Immigrants had to stop at Ellis Island before they could enter the United States. Their ships passed the Statue of Liberty. The statue was a welcome sight for the people. It represented their new country and its freedom.

Ellis Island was the first stop for many people who came to the United States.

The statue's hand holds a tablet with the date of America's birthday — July 4, 1776.

The Statue of Liberty is still a grand statue. The body is taller than a building with twelve floors. Each hand is longer than two cars. Each finger is taller than a person. One fingernail is wider than this book.

Statue of Liberty Facts

Total height, from base to torch:	305 feet 1 inch (93 meters)
Height from feet to top of torch:	151 feet 1 inch (46 m)
Heel to top of head:	111 feet, 1 inch (34 m)
Length of hand:	16 feet, 5 inches (5 m)
Length of nose:	4 feet 6 inches (1.4 m)
Width of an eye:	2 feet 6 inches (.8 m)
Right arm length:	42 feet (12.8 m)
Height of the torch:	21 feet (6.4 m)
Height from chin to top of head:	17 feet 3 inches (5.2 m)
Width of mouth:	3 feet (.9 m)
Index finger:	8 feet (2.4 m)

The statue's copper skin turned
green over time.

Some things have changed over the years. When
the Statue of Liberty first came to New York, it was
the color of a penny. Over time, the damp ocean
air turned the copper light green.

The first torch was solid copper. In 1916, workers cut windows in the torch. They put lamps inside. At night, the torch looked like a flame. In the 1980s, the statue was given a new torch. The new torch is painted gold.

For many years, the statue's torch had windows.

Visitors take a ferry to reach
Liberty Island.

Visiting the Statue of Liberty

People can take a ferry to Liberty Island. They
can tour the grounds. They can see how large
the statue is. Visitors can also take a ferry to
Ellis Island. There, they can learn about the many
people who have moved to the United States.

The Statue of Liberty is known all over the world. It is a beautiful symbol of freedom. The statue is also a symbol of the United States. The statue and the country offer hope to people who are not free.

The Statue of Liberty is a powerful symbol of freedom.

Glossary

copper — a reddish metal that bends easily

crate — a box made of wood

immigrant — a person who comes to another country to live

independence — freedom

liberty — freedom

represent — to be a symbol of something

site — the place where a statue or building stands

skeleton — a frame that supports a body or object

torch — a light or flame

unveiled — shown for the first time

For More Information

Books

Binns, Tristan Boyer. *The Statue of Liberty*. Chicago: Heinemann Library, 2001.

Curlee, Lynn. *Liberty*. New York: Atheneum Books for Young Readers, 2000.

Deady, Kathleen W. *The Statue of Liberty*. Mankato: Bridgestone Books, 2002.

Web Sites

American Icon: Lady Liberty
travel.discovery.com/convergence/americanicon/
ladyliberty/statue.html
An interactive site with fun facts about the statue and a tour of Ellis Island

National Geographic Kids: The Light of Liberty
www.nationalgeographic.com/ngkids/9907/liberty
Photos and facts

PBS Kids: Learning Adventures in Citizenship
www.pbs.org/wnet/newyork/laic/episode3/topic2/
e3_topic2.html
Photos, facts, and activities

Index

About the Author

Susan Ashley has written over eighteen books for
children, including two picture books about dogs, *Puppy
Love* and *When I'm Happy, I Smile*. She enjoys animals
and writing about them. Susan lives in Wisconsin with
her husband and two frisky felines.